I0009456

Module 1: Introduction to Web Programming

1.1 What is a Web App?

A Web App (or web application) is a program that runs on a server and is accessed through a web browser. Web Apps offer functionalities similar to applications installed on a computer (such as Microsoft Word or Adobe Photoshop) but are accessible via the Internet, without needing to be downloaded or installed.

Example of a Web App

- **Gmail**: An email service you can use in the browser to read and send emails.
- **Google Docs**: An online text editor that allows you to write and edit documents directly in the browser.

Difference Between Static Websites and Web Apps

- **Static Website**: A simple website, such as a business information page, where the content does not change unless manually updated.
- **Dynamic Web App**: An application that responds to user actions, like an online shopping cart that updates selected products in real time.

1.2 Difference Between Front-End and Back-End

The world of web programming is divided into two main parts: **Front-End** and **Back-End**. Both are necessary to make a Web App functional.

Front-End (Client Side)

The Front-End is everything that the user can see and interact with directly in the browser. It is the visible part of a Web App, composed of:

- **HTML (HyperText Markup Language)**: Defines the structure of the page (titles, paragraphs, images, etc.).

- **CSS (Cascading Style Sheets)**: Adds style to the page (colors, layouts, fonts, etc.).

- **JavaScript**: Adds interactivity to the page (dropdown menus, dynamic forms, animations, etc.).

Example of Front-End

Imagine opening an e-commerce website. Everything you see — product images, buttons, text, and the general layout — is managed by the Front-End.

```
<!DOCTYPE html>
<html>
  <head>
    <title>Online Store</title>
    <style>
      h1 { color: blue; }
      p { font-size: 16px; }
    </style>
  </head>
  <body>
    <h1>Welcome to Our Store!</h1>
    <p>Here you can shop for the best products.</p>
  </body>
</html>
```

In this example, **HTML** creates the structure of the page, and **CSS** adds the style.

Back-End (Server Side)

The Back-End is everything that happens behind the scenes of the Web App. It is the part not visible to users and handles:

- **Data Processing**: Performs calculations or actions necessary for the app to function.
- **Database**: Stores and retrieves information, such as user details or products in a catalog.
- **Authentication**: Verifies user credentials (for example, when logging into a site).

Common programming languages for the Back-End include **PHP**, **Python**, **Ruby**, **Node.js**, and **Java**.

Example of Back-End

When you log into a website, the Back-End processes the information, compares it with the database, and decides whether to grant or deny access.

1.3 Client-Server Architecture

To understand how a Web App works, it is essential to grasp the concept of Client-Server architecture.

Client

The **Client** is the device used by the user to access the Web App, such as a computer, tablet, or smartphone. The client sends requests to the server to obtain information or perform actions.

Example: When you type a URL into a browser, you are sending a request to the server to display a webpage.

Server

The **Server** is a powerful computer that receives requests from the client, processes the information, and sends a response. The server can provide HTML pages, manage databases, or perform complex operations.

Example: When you access a video streaming site, the server sends the video data to your device so you can watch it.

Practical Example of Client-Server Communication

1. Open a browser and type the address of a website (e.g., www.example.com).
2. The browser (client) sends a request to the server of example.com.
3. The server receives the request, retrieves the required data, and sends it back to the client.
4. The browser displays the data as a webpage.

1.4 Essential Tools for Web Development

To start developing Web Apps, you need some basic tools:

1. Text Editor

A text editor is a program used to write code. Here are some popular editors:
- **Visual Studio Code**: One of the most widely used editors by developers. It includes many advanced features, such as code auto-completion.
- **Sublime Text**: Lightweight and highly customizable.
- **Atom**: An open-source editor with a wide range of extensions.

2. Web Browser

A web browser like **Google Chrome**, **Firefox**, or **Safari** is used to view Web Apps and test the code. Modern browsers have built-in **Developer Tools** that allow you to:
- Inspect HTML and CSS code.
- Debug JavaScript.
- Monitor network requests.

3. Console

The console is a tool that allows you to execute commands or debug directly in the browser. It is useful for viewing error messages and testing small JavaScript snippets.

Example: Open the console in Google Chrome with `Ctrl + Shift + J` (or `Cmd + Option + J` on Mac) and type:

```
console.log('Hello World!');
```

You will see the message **"Hello World!"** displayed in the console.

Installing Visual Studio Code

1. Download and install **Visual Studio Code** from code.visualstudio.com.
2. Open the editor and create a new file named `index.html`.
3. Write a simple HTML code, save it, and open it in your browser to see the result.

Module 2: HTML - Basic and Advanced Structure

2.1 Basic Structure of an HTML Page

HTML (HyperText Markup Language) is the basic language used to create web pages. Every HTML page follows a well-defined structure.

Basic Structure

Here is an example of a basic HTML page:

```html
<!DOCTYPE html>
<html lang="it">
  <head>
    <meta charset="UTF-8">
    <meta http-equiv="X-UA-Compatible" content="IE=edge">
    <meta name="viewport" content="width=device-width, initial-scale=1.0">
    <title>My First Web Page</title>
  </head>
  <body>
    <h1>Hello World!</h1>
    <p>Welcome to my first web page.</p>
  </body>
</html>
```

Explanation of Fundamental Elements

- `<!DOCTYPE html>`: This is the document type declaration and tells the browser that HTML5 is being used.
- `<html lang="it">`: Root tag that wraps all HTML content. The `lang="it"` attribute specifies that the content is in Italian.
- `<head>`: Contains information (metadata) about the page, such as the title, keywords for search engines, and links to CSS files.
- `<meta charset="UTF-8">`: Specifies the character set used, in this case, UTF-8, which supports most characters.
- `<title>`: Defines the title of the page that appears in the browser tab.
- `<body>`: Contains all the visible content of the page, such as text, images, links, etc.
- `<h1>`: Main heading tag, used for important titles.
- `<p>`: Paragraph tag, used for blocks of text.

2.2 Semantic Tags and Advanced HTML

HTML provides semantic tags that improve code organization and readability, making it easier to understand the purpose of each section.

Introduction to Semantic Tags

Semantic tags describe the content they enclose, helping both developers and search engines better understand the structure of the page.

- `<header>`: Introductory section of the page or a section.
- `<nav>`: Contains navigation links.
- `<section>`: Thematic section of the document.
- `<article>`: Self-contained, reusable content, such as a news article.
- `<aside>`: Marginal or related content, such as a sidebar.
- `<footer>`: Footer of the document or a section.

Example of a Page with Semantic Tags

```
<!DOCTYPE html>
<html lang="it">
  <head>
    <meta charset="UTF-8">
    <title>Page with Semantic Tags</title>
  </head>
  <body>
    <header>
      <h1>Welcome to Our Website</h1>
      <nav>
        <a href="#home">Home</a>
        <a href="#articles">Articles</a>
        <a href="#contacts">Contacts</a>
      </nav>
    </header>
    <main>
      <section id="articles">
        <article>
          <h2>Article 1</h2>
          <p>This is the content of the first article.</p>
        </article>
        <article>
          <h2>Article 2</h2>
```

```html
        <p>This is the content of the second article.</p>
      </article>
    </section>
    <aside>
      <h3>Useful Resources</h3>
      <ul>
        <li><a href="#">Link 1</a></li>
        <li><a href="#">Link 2</a></li>
      </ul>
    </aside>
  </main>
  <footer>
    <p>Copyright © 2024. All rights reserved.</p>
  </footer>
  </body>
</html>
```

Tables, Forms, and Inputs

Tables

Tables are used to display data in a tabular format.

```html
<table>
  <tr>
    <th>Name</th>
    <th>Age</th>
  </tr>
  <tr>
    <td>Mario</td>
    <td>25</td>
  </tr>
  <tr>
    <td>Luigi</td>
    <td>30</td>
  </tr>
</table>
```

- **`<table>`**: Defines a table.
- **`<tr>`**: Defines a row in the table.
- **`<th>`**: Defines a header cell (in bold).
- **`<td>`**: Defines a data cell.

Forms and Inputs

Forms are used to collect data from users.

```
<form action="/submit-data" method="post">
  <label for="name">Name:</label>
  <input type="text" id="name" name="name">
  <label for="email">Email:</label>
  <input type="email" id="email" name="email">
  <button type="submit">Submit</button>
</form>
```

- **`<form>`**: Creates a form for data submission.
- **`<input>`**: Defines a generic input field for the user.
- **`<button>`**: Button to submit the form.

Embedding Multimedia: Images, Videos, and Audio

Images: Use the `<img>` tag to insert images.

```
<img src="image.jpg" alt="Image description">
```

Videos: Use the `<video>` tag to embed videos.

```
<video controls>
<source src="video.mp4" type="video/mp4">
Your browser does not support the video element.
</video>
```

Audio: Use the `<audio>` tag to embed audio.

```
<audio controls>
<source src="audio.mp3" type="audio/mpeg">
Your browser does not support the audio element.
</audio>
```

2.3 All HTML Tags

1. Basic Structure Tags

- `<!DOCTYPE>`: Declares the version of HTML.
- `<html>`: Root tag that encloses all HTML content.
- `<head>`: Contains metadata and links to external resources.
- `<title>`: Defines the title of the page.
- `<meta>`: Provides metadata about the page.
- `<link>`: Links external resources, such as CSS files.
- `<style>`: Adds internal CSS styles.
- `<body>`: Contains all visible content of the page.
- `<base>`: Specifies the base URL for relative links.

2. Text and Formatting Tags

- `<h1>` to `<h6>`: Headings of varying levels, from `<h1>` (largest) to `<h6>` (smallest).
- `<p>`: Defines a paragraph.
- `<br>`: Adds a line break.
- `<hr>`: Adds a horizontal line.
- `<strong>`: Makes text bold for emphasis.
- `<em>`: Italicizes text for emphasis.
- `<b>`: Makes text bold (without semantic emphasis).
- `<i>`: Italicizes text (without semantic emphasis).
- `<u>`: Underlines text.
- `<mark>`: Highlights text.
- `<small>`: Makes text smaller.
- `<del>`: Displays text as deleted.
- `<ins>`: Displays text as inserted (underlined).
- `<sub>`: Makes text subscript.
- `<sup>`: Makes text superscript.
- `<blockquote>`: Defines a long quotation.
- `<q>`: Defines a short inline quotation.
- `<cite>`: Represents the title of a work.
- `<abbr>`: Defines an abbreviation or acronym.
- `<address>`: Provides contact information.
- `<bdo>`: Changes text direction.
- `<code>`: Displays text as code.
- `<pre>`: Displays text with preserved spacing.
- `<kbd>`: Represents keyboard input.
- `<samp>`: Represents program output.
- `<var>`: Represents a variable.

3. Linking and Image Tags

- `<a>`: Creates a hyperlink.
- `<img>`: Inserts an image.
- `<map>`: Defines an image map.
- `<area>`: Defines an area within an image map.
- `<figure>`: Groups multimedia content with captions.
- `<figcaption>`: Adds a caption to `<figure>`.

4. List Tags

- `<ul>`: Creates an unordered list.
- `<ol>`: Creates an ordered list.
- `<li>`: Defines a list item.
- `<dl>`: Creates a definition list.
- `<dt>`: Defines a term in a definition list.
- `<dd>`: Defines a description for the term.

5. Table Tags

- `<table>`: Defines a table.
- `<tr>`: Defines a row in the table.
- `<td>`: Defines a data cell.
- `<th>`: Defines a header cell.
- `<caption>`: Adds a caption to the table.
- `<colgroup>`: Groups columns in a table.
- `<col>`: Defines properties for a column.
- `<thead>`: Groups the header content in a table.
- `<tbody>`: Groups the body content in a table.
- `<tfoot>`: Groups the footer content in a table.

6. Semantic Tags

- `<header>`: Defines the header of a page or section.
- `<nav>`: Contains navigation links.
- `<section>`: Defines a thematic section.
- `<article>`: Represents self-contained, reusable content.
- `<aside>`: Related or marginal content.
- `<footer>`: Defines the footer of a document or section.
- `<main>`: Represents the main content of a page.
- `<figure>`: Groups multimedia content with captions.
- `<figcaption>`: Caption for `<figure>`.
- `<time>`: Represents a date or time.
- `<details>`: Provides interactive details that users can expand or collapse.
- `<summary>`: Summary for `<details>`.
- `<mark>`: Highlights text.

7. Form and Input Tags

- `<form>`: Creates a form for data submission.
- `<input>`: Defines a generic input field.
- `<label>`: Labels an input field.
- `<button>`: Creates a clickable button.
- `<select>`: Creates a dropdown menu.
- `<option>`: Defines an option in a dropdown menu.
- `<textarea>`: Creates a multi-line text field.
- `<fieldset>`: Groups related input fields.
- `<legend>`: Provides a caption for `<fieldset>`.
- `<datalist>`: Defines a list of predefined options for an input.
- `<output>`: Represents the result of a calculation.
- `<progress>`: Displays the progress of a task.
- `<meter>`: Represents a scalar measurement within a known range.

8. Multimedia Tags

- `<audio>`: Adds audio content.
- `<video>`: Adds video content.
- `<source>`: Specifies multiple resources for multimedia elements.
- `<track>`: Adds subtitles to videos.
- `<embed>`: Embeds external content.
- `<object>`: Embeds an external object.
- `<param>`: Specifies parameters for `<object>`.
- `<iframe>`: Embeds another webpage.

9. Script and Metadata Tags

- `<script>`: Adds JavaScript to the page.
- `<noscript>`: Provides alternative content if JavaScript is disabled.
- `<template>`: Defines reusable HTML content.
- `<slot>`: Used with Web Components for custom content insertion.

Module 3: CSS - Basic and Advanced Styling

3.1 What is CSS?

CSS (Cascading Style Sheets) is a language used to describe the presentation and style of a document written in HTML. CSS allows control over the appearance of a web page, managing colors, layouts, fonts, margins, spacing, and much more.

What is CSS used for?

- **Styling**: Modifies the appearance of HTML content, such as changing colors, font sizes, and layouts.
- **Separation of Content and Style**: Keeps HTML content separate from styling, making the code cleaner and easier to manage.
- **Improved User Experience**: Enables the creation of responsive layouts that adapt to different devices (desktop, tablet, smartphone).
- **Code Optimization**: Reduces the amount of HTML code needed for styling, improving website performance.

Ways to Use CSS

There are three main ways to use CSS:

1. Inline CSS
Inline CSS is written directly inside an HTML element using the style attribute.

```
<p style="color: red; font-size: 20px;">Text with inline style</p>
```

- **Advantage**: Useful for quickly styling an element.
- **Disadvantage**: Difficult to manage for large or complex web pages.

2. Internal CSS

Internal CSS is defined inside a `<style>` tag in the `<head>` section of an HTML document.

```html
<!DOCTYPE html>
<html lang="it">
  <head>
    <style>
      h1 {
        color: blue;
        text-align: center;
      }
    </style>
  </head>
  <body>
    <h1>Welcome</h1>
  </body>
</html>
```

- **Advantage**: Useful for styling a single web page.
- **Disadvantage**: Not efficient for styling multiple pages.

3. External CSS

External CSS is written in a separate file with a `.css` extension and linked to the HTML page using the `<link>` tag.

```html
<!DOCTYPE html>
<html lang="it">
  <head>
    <link rel="stylesheet" href="style.css">
  </head>
  <body>
    <h1>Hello World!</h1>
  </body>
</html>
```

- **Advantage**: Ideal for styling multiple pages uniformly and keeping the code clean.
- **Disadvantage**: Requires managing multiple files.

3.2 Basic CSS

Selectors, Properties, and Values

- **Selectors**: Identify the HTML elements to which the style is applied.
- **Properties**: Specify the aspect to be modified (e.g., color, font, margin).
- **Values**: Define how the property is applied (e.g., red, 16px, bold).

Example of a CSS Rule

```
p {
  color: green; /* Color property with value green */
  font-size: 16px; /* Font size */
}
```

Colors, Fonts, Spacing, and Box Model

- **Colors**: Defined with names (red), HEX values (#ff0000), RGB (rgb(255, 0, 0)), or HSL (hsl(0, 100%, 50%)).
- **Fonts**: Properties control the font type, size, style, and weight.
- **Spacing**: Margins and padding manage the space between and within elements.
- **Box Model**: Defines how the space occupied by an element is calculated, including content, padding, border, and margin.

3.3 Advanced CSS

Layouts with Flexbox and Grid

- **Flexbox**: A layout system that simplifies the alignment of elements in rows or columns.

Example:

```
.container {
  display: flex;
  justify-content: center;
  align-items: center;
}
```

- **CSS Grid**: A grid layout system that allows organizing elements in rows and columns.

Example:

```
.grid-container {
  display: grid;
  grid-template-columns: 1fr 1fr;
  gap: 20px;
}
```

Transitions and Animations

- **Transitions**: Create gradual changes in properties.

Example:

```
.box {
  transition: background-color 0.5s;
}

.box:hover {
  background-color: lightblue;
}
```

- **Animations**: Define sequences of changes using @keyframes.

Example:

```
@keyframes fade {
  from { opacity: 0; }
  to { opacity: 1; }
}

.fade-in {
  animation: fade 2s;
}
```

Pseudo-classes and Pseudo-elements

- **Pseudo-classes**: Apply styles based on a particular state (e.g., :hover).

Example: Change the color of a link when hovered over.

```
a:hover {
  color: orange;
}
```

- **Pseudo-elements**: Style a specific part of an element (e.g., ::before).

Example: Add content before an element.

```
p::before {
  content: "Note: ";
  font-weight: bold;
}
```

Media Queries for Responsive Layouts

Media Queries allow styles to be applied based on screen size, making web pages responsive.

Example of a Media Query

```
@media (max-width: 600px) {
  body {
    font-size: 14px;
  }
}
```

3.4 All CSS Selectors and Properties

CSS Selectors

Type Selector: Selects all elements of a specific type.

```
p { color: blue; }
```

Class Selector: Selects elements with a specific class.

```
.class { background-color: yellow; }
```

ID Selector: Selects an element with a specific ID.

```
#id { border: 1px solid black; }
```

Universal Selector: Selects all elements.

```
* { margin: 0; padding: 0; }
```

Descendant Selector: Selects elements that are descendants of another element.

```
div p { font-style: italic; }
```

Attribute Selector: Selects elements with a specific attribute.

```
a[target="_blank"] { color: red; }
```

Properties by Category

1. Color and Background Properties

- `color`: Defines text color.
- `background-color`: Sets the background color of an element.
- `background-image`: Sets a background image.
- `background-position`: Specifies the position of a background image.
- `background-size`: Specifies the size of a background image.
- `background-repeat`: Determines if and how the background image is repeated.
- `background-attachment`: Specifies whether the background image scrolls or remains fixed.
- `background-clip`: Specifies the painting area of the background color.
- `background-origin`: Specifies the origin point of the background image.
- `background`: Shorthand property for all background properties.

2. Text Properties

- `font-family`: Specifies the font type.
- `font-size`: Sets the font size.
- `font-weight`: Specifies font weight (e.g., bold, normal).
- `font-style`: Specifies text style (e.g., italic, normal).
- `line-height`: Specifies line height.
- `text-align`: Aligns text (e.g., left, right, center).
- `text-decoration`: Adds text decorations (e.g., underline, line-through).
- `text-transform`: Controls text capitalization (e.g., uppercase).
- `letter-spacing`: Sets spacing between characters.
- `word-spacing`: Sets spacing between words.

3. Layout Properties

- `display`: Specifies how to display an element (e.g., block, inline, flex).
- `position`: Specifies the positioning method (e.g., static, relative, absolute).
- `z-index`: Specifies the stack order of elements.

4. Transition and Animation Properties

- `transition`: Shorthand for defining transitions.
- `animation`: Shorthand for defining animations.

5. Flexbox and Grid Properties

- `display: flex`: Activates the Flexbox layout.
- `justify-content`: Aligns items along the main axis.
- `display: grid`: Activates the Grid layout.
- `grid-template-columns`: Defines grid columns.
- `grid-template`: Shorthand property for grid-template-rows, grid-template-columns, and `grid-template-areas`.
- `grid-column:` Shorthand property for `grid-column-start` and `grid-column-end`.
- `grid-row:` Shorthand property `for grid-row-start and grid-row-end`. `grid-area:` Specifies a grid `area`.
- `grid-auto-rows:` Defines the automatic height of rows.
- `grid-auto-columns:` Defines the automatic width of columns. grid-auto-flow: `Specifies how items are automatically placed in the grid`.
- `gap: Specifies the space between rows and columns`.
- `row-gap:` Space `between rows`.
- `column-gap:` Space between columns.

Module 4: JavaScript - Logic and Interactivity

JavaScript is a programming language that allows web pages to be interactive. It runs in the user's browser and is essential for developing dynamic web applications.

4.1 Basic JavaScript

Syntax and Variables

- **Syntax**: JavaScript uses a syntax similar to other programming languages. Statements are terminated with a semicolon (;), though it is not always mandatory.

Variables: Used to store data. Declared using var, let, or const.

```
var name = "Mario"; // Variable declared with var
let age = 25;        // Variable declared with let
const PI = 3.14;     // Constant declared with const
```

Data Types and Operators

- **Primitive Data Types**: string, number, boolean, null, undefined, symbol.
- **Complex Data Types**: object (including arrays, functions, objects).
- **Operators**:

  ○ Arithmetic Operators: +, -, *, /, %.
  ○ Assignment Operators: =, +=, -=, *=, /=.
  ○ Comparison Operators: ==, ===, !=, !==, >, <, >=, <=.
  ○ Logical Operators: &&, ||, !.

Example:

```
let a = 5;
let b = 10;
let sum = a + b; // 15
```

Functions and Scope

Functions: Block of code that performs a specific operation. It can accept parameters and return a value.

```
function greet(name) {
return "Hello, " + name + "!";
}
console.log(greet("Marco")); // "Hello, Marco!"
```

- **Scope**: Refers to the visibility of a variable.
  - Local Scope: Variables declared inside a function.
  - Global Scope: Variables declared outside a function.

Example:

```
let name = "Anna"; // Global variable

function showName() {
  let localName = "Luca"; // Local variable
  console.log(localName);
}

showName(); // "Luca"
console.log(name); // "Anna"
```

DOM Manipulation (Document Object Model)

The DOM represents the structure of a web page. JavaScript can be used to manipulate HTML elements.
- **Selecting Elements**:
  - document.getElementById: Selects an element by ID.
  - document.querySelector: Selects the first element matching a CSS selector.

```
let title = document.getElementById("title");
let paragraph = document.querySelector(".paragraph");
```

- **Modifying Content**:

  - `element.textContent`: Changes the text of an element.
  - `element.innerHTML`: Changes the HTML content of an element.

```
  title.textContent = "New Title";
paragraph.innerHTML = "<strong>Modified Text</strong>";
```

- **Adding and Removing Elements**:

  - `element.appendChild`: Adds a new child node.
  - `element.remove`: Removes an element.

4.2 Advanced JavaScript

Events and User Action Handling

- **Events**: JavaScript can detect events, such as clicks or mouse movements.

`element.addEventListener`: Adds an event listener.

```javascript
  let button = document.querySelector("button");
button.addEventListener("click", function() {
  alert("Button clicked!");
});
```

Promises and Asynchronous Code with async/await

Promises: Objects that represent the completion (or failure) of an asynchronous operation.

```javascript
  let promise = new Promise(function(resolve, reject) {
  let success = true;
  if (success) {
    resolve("Operation completed");
  } else {
    reject("Error");
  }
});

promise.then(function(message) {
  console.log(message);
}).catch(function(error) {
  console.log(error);
});
```

Async/Await: Simpler syntax for working with asynchronous code.

```
async function fetchData() {
try {
  let response = await fetch("https://api.example.com/data");
  let data = await response.json();
  console.log(data);
} catch (error) {
  console.error("Error:", error);
}
}
fetchData();
```

Working with APIs and Fetch

Fetch: Method for making HTTP requests to retrieve data from a server.

```
fetch("https://api.example.com/data")
.then(response => response.json())
.then(data => console.log(data))
.catch(error => console.error("Error:", error));
```

Introduction to Libraries and Frameworks (e.g., jQuery)

jQuery: A JavaScript library that simplifies DOM manipulation and event handling.

```
$(document).ready(function() {
$("#button").click(function() {
  $("p").text("Text modified with jQuery");
});
});
```

4.3 Complete List of JavaScript Functions and Objects

Basic Functions and Methods

- `console.log()`: Prints a message to the console.
- `alert()`: Displays an alert to the user.
- `parseInt()`: Converts a string to an integer.
- `parseFloat()`: Converts a string to a decimal number.
- `isNaN()`: Checks if a value is not a number.
- `typeof`: Returns the type of a variable.

Built-in Objects

- **Math**: Object for mathematical operations.
  - `Math.random()`: Returns a random number between 0 and 1.
  - `Math.floor()`: Rounds a number down.
- **Date**: Object for handling dates and times.
  - `new Date()`: Creates a new date object.
  - `date.getFullYear()`: Returns the year.

Array Properties and Methods

- `push()`: Adds an element to the end of an array.
- `pop()`: Removes the last element of an array.
- `shift()`: Removes the first element of an array.
- `unshift()`: Adds an element to the beginning of an array.
- `forEach()`: Executes a function for each element in the array.
- `map()`: Creates a new array with the results of a function applied to each element.
- `filter()`: Creates a new array with elements that meet a condition.

String Properties and Methods

- `length`: Returns the length of a string.
- `toUpperCase()`: Converts a string to uppercase.
- `toLowerCase()`: Converts a string to lowercase.
- `charAt()`: Returns the character at a specific index.
- `split()`: Splits a string into an array of substrings.
- `replace()`: Replaces a substring with another.

Module 5: SQL and MySQL - Data Management

SQL (Structured Query Language) is a language used to manage and manipulate databases. **MySQL** is one of the most popular relational database management systems, which uses SQL to perform data operations.

5.1 Basic SQL

Syntax and Main Commands

SELECT: Retrieves data from one or more tables.

Syntax:

```
SELECT column1, column2 FROM table;
```

Example:

```
SELECT name, age FROM users;
```

INSERT: Inserts new data into a table.

Syntax:

```
INSERT INTO table (column1, column2) VALUES (value1, value2);
```

Example:

```
INSERT INTO users (name, age) VALUES ('Mario', 30);
```

UPDATE: Updates existing data in a table.

Syntax:

```
UPDATE table SET column1 = value1 WHERE condition;
```

Example:

```
UPDATE users SET age = 31 WHERE name = 'Mario';
```

DELETE: Deletes data from a table.

Syntax:

```
DELETE FROM table WHERE condition;
```

Example:

```
DELETE FROM users WHERE name = 'Mario';
```

Filtering and Sorting Operators

WHERE: Filters data based on a condition.

Example:

```
SELECT * FROM users WHERE age > 25;
```

AND, OR, NOT: Logical operators for combining conditions.

Example:

```
SELECT * FROM users WHERE age > 25 AND city = 'Rome';
```

ORDER BY: Sorts results in ascending or descending order.

Example:

```
SELECT * FROM users ORDER BY age DESC;
```

LIMIT: Limits the number of returned results.

Example:

```
SELECT * FROM users LIMIT 5;
```

5.2 Advanced SQL

Joins, Subqueries, and Aggregate Functions

- **JOIN**: Combines data from multiple tables based on a relationship.

INNER JOIN: Returns rows with matches in both tables.

```
  SELECT users.name, orders.date
FROM users
INNER JOIN orders ON users.id = orders.user_id;
```

LEFT JOIN: Returns all rows from the left table and matching rows from the right table.

```
  SELECT users.name, orders.date
FROM users
LEFT JOIN orders ON users.id = orders.user_id;
```

Subquery: A query within another query.

Example:

```
SELECT name FROM users WHERE age = (SELECT MAX(age) FROM users);
```

- **Aggregate Functions**: Perform calculations on a set of values and return a single value.

COUNT: Counts the number of rows.

```
  SELECT COUNT(*) FROM users;
```

SUM: Sums the values of a column.

```
  SELECT SUM(price) FROM orders;
```

AVG: Calculates the average of values.

```
  SELECT AVG(age) FROM users;
```

MAX and MIN: Return the maximum and minimum values.

```
  SELECT MAX(age), MIN(age) FROM users;
```

Stored Procedures and Triggers

Stored Procedures: A set of SQL instructions that can be saved and executed.
Example:

```sql
CREATE PROCEDURE UpdateAge (IN user_id INT, IN new_age INT)
BEGIN
  UPDATE users SET age = new_age WHERE id = user_id;
END;
```

Triggers: Automatic actions executed when an event occurs on a table.
Example:

```sql
CREATE TRIGGER after_insert
AFTER INSERT ON users
FOR EACH ROW
BEGIN
  INSERT INTO log (action, date) VALUES ('New user added', NOW());
END;
```

5.3 MySQL and Relational Databases

Installing and Configuring MySQL

- **Installation**: Download and install MySQL from the official website.
- **Basic Configuration**:
  - Set up the root user and permissions.
  - Start the MySQL server and access it via the MySQL client.

Creating and Managing Databases, Tables, and Relationships

Create a Database:

```
CREATE DATABASE database_name;
```

Create a Table:

```
CREATE TABLE users (
id INT AUTO_INCREMENT PRIMARY KEY,
name VARCHAR(50),
age INT
);
```

Add Relationships: Use foreign keys to define relationships between tables.

```
CREATE TABLE orders (
id INT AUTO_INCREMENT PRIMARY KEY,
user_id INT,
date DATE,
FOREIGN KEY (user_id) REFERENCES users(id)
);
```

5.4 All SQL Commands and Functions

Here is a structured list of the main SQL commands and functions.

Main SQL Commands

DDL (Data Definition Language):

- **CREATE:** Creates a new database or table.

  ```sql
  CREATE TABLE users (id INT, name VARCHAR(50));
  ```

- **ALTER:** Modifies an existing table.

  ```sql
  ALTER TABLE users ADD column VARCHAR(50);
  ```

- **DROP:** Deletes a database or a table.

  ```sql
  DROP TABLE users;
  ```

DML (Data Manipulation Language):

- **SELECT:** Retrieves data from a table.

  ```sql
  SELECT * FROM users;
  ```

- **INSERT:** Inserts new data into a table.

  ```sql
  INSERT INTO users (name, age) VALUES ('Luca', 28);
  ```

- **UPDATE:** Updates existing data in a table.

  ```sql
  UPDATE users SET age = 29 WHERE name = 'Luca';
  ```

- **DELETE:** Deletes data from a table.

  ```sql
  DELETE FROM users WHERE name = 'Luca';
  ```

DCL (Data Control Language):

- **GRANT:** Grants permissions to a user.

```
GRANT ALL PRIVILEGES ON database.* TO 'user'@'localhost';
```

- **REVOKE:** Revokes permissions from a user.

```
REVOKE ALL PRIVILEGES ON database.* FROM 'user'@'localhost';
```

TCL (Transaction Control Language):

- **COMMIT:** Confirms a transaction.
- **ROLLBACK:** Cancels a transaction.
- **SAVEPOINT:** Sets a save point within a transaction.

Aggregate Functions

These functions perform calculations on a set of values and return a single value.
- **COUNT():** Counts the number of rows matching a condition.

```
SELECT COUNT(*) FROM users;
```

- **SUM():** Sums the values of a numeric column.

```
SELECT SUM(price) FROM products;
```

- **AVG():** Calculates the average of a numeric column.

```
SELECT AVG(salary) FROM employees;
```

- **MAX():** Returns the maximum value in a column.

```
SELECT MAX(age) FROM users;
```

- **MIN():** Returns the minimum value in a column.

```
SELECT MIN(price) FROM products;
```

String Functions

These functions manipulate textual data.

- **CONCAT():** Combines two or more strings.

  ```sql
  SELECT CONCAT(first_name, ' ', last_name) AS full_name FROM
  users;
  ```

- **SUBSTRING():** Extracts part of a string.

  ```sql
  SELECT SUBSTRING(name, 1, 3) FROM users; -- First 3 characters
  ```

- **CHAR_LENGTH():** Returns the length of a string.

  ```sql
  SELECT CHAR_LENGTH(name) FROM users;
  ```

- **UPPER():** Converts a string to uppercase.

  ```sql
  SELECT UPPER(name) FROM users;
  ```

- **LOWER():** Converts a string to lowercase.

  ```sql
  SELECT LOWER(last_name) FROM users;
  ```

- **TRIM():** Removes leading and trailing whitespace from a string.

  ```sql
  SELECT TRIM(name) FROM users;
  ```

- **REPLACE():** Replaces a substring with another within a string.

  ```sql
  SELECT REPLACE(name, 'a', 'o') FROM users;
  ```

- **LPAD():** Pads the start of a string with a specific character to reach a certain length.

  ```sql
  SELECT LPAD(number, 5, '0') FROM numbers; -- Adds zeros up to
  5 digits
  ```

- **RPAD():** Pads the end of a string with a specific character to reach a certain length.

  ```sql
  SELECT RPAD(name, 10, '*') FROM users;
  ```

- **INSTR():** Returns the position of the first occurrence of a substring in a string.

```
SELECT INSTR(name, 'a') FROM users; -- Position of 'a' in the
string
```

- **LEFT():** Returns a specified number of characters from the start of a string.

```
SELECT LEFT(name, 2) FROM users; -- First 2 characters
```

- **RIGHT():** Returns a specified number of characters from the end of a string.

```
SELECT RIGHT(name, 2) FROM users; -- Last 2 characters
```

Date and Time Functions

These functions handle date and time operations.
- **NOW():** Returns the current date and time.

```
SELECT NOW();
```

- **CURDATE():** Returns the current date.

```
SELECT CURDATE();
```

- **CURTIME():** Returns the current time.

```
SELECT CURTIME();
```

- **DATE():** Extracts the date part from a datetime value.

```
SELECT DATE(created_at) FROM orders;
```

- **YEAR():** Extracts the year from a date.

```
SELECT YEAR(birth_date) FROM users;
```

- **MONTH():** Extracts the month from a date.

```
SELECT MONTH(birth_date) FROM users;
```

- **DAY():** Extracts the day from a date.

```
SELECT DAY(birth_date) FROM users;
```

- **HOUR():** Extracts the hour from a datetime value.

```sql
SELECT HOUR(created_at) FROM orders;
```

- **MINUTE():** Extracts the minutes from a datetime value.

```sql
SELECT MINUTE(created_at) FROM orders;
```

- **SECOND():** Extracts the seconds from a datetime value.

```sql
SELECT SECOND(created_at) FROM orders;
```

- **DATEDIFF():** Calculates the difference between two dates.

```sql
SELECT DATEDIFF('2024-12-31', '2024-01-01');
```

- **DATE_ADD():** Adds an interval to a date.

```sql
SELECT DATE_ADD(created_at, INTERVAL 10 DAY) FROM orders;
```

- **DATE_SUB():** Subtracts an interval from a date.

```sql
SELECT DATE_SUB(created_at, INTERVAL 5 DAY) FROM orders;
```

Mathematical Functions

These functions perform mathematical operations.

- **ABS():** Returns the absolute value of a number.

```sql
SELECT ABS(-10);
```

- **CEIL():** Rounds a number up to the nearest integer.

```sql
SELECT CEIL(10.3); -- Returns 11
```

- **FLOOR():** Rounds a number down to the nearest integer.

```sql
SELECT FLOOR(10.7); -- Returns 10
```

- **ROUND():** Rounds a number to a specified number of decimal places.

```sql
SELECT ROUND(123.456, 2); -- Returns 123.46
```

- **MOD():** Returns the remainder of a division.

```
SELECT MOD(10, 3); -- Returns 1
```

- **POWER():** Raises a number to a power.

```
SELECT POWER(2, 3); -- Returns 8
```

- **SQRT():** Returns the square root of a number.

```
SELECT SQRT(16); -- Returns 4
```

- **RAND():** Returns a random number between 0 and 1.

```
SELECT RAND();
```

Control Flow Functions

These functions control the logical flow of queries.
- **IF():** Returns a value based on a condition.

```
SELECT IF(age >= 18, 'Adult', 'Minor') FROM users;
```

- **CASE:** Executes conditional instructions similar to a switch structure.

```
SELECT
CASE
  WHEN age < 18 THEN 'Minor'
  WHEN age BETWEEN 18 AND 65 THEN 'Adult'
  ELSE 'Senior'
END AS category
FROM users;
```

This list covers the main SQL functions used for managing and manipulating data in databases.

Module 6: Python - Basic and Advanced Programming

Python is a high-level programming language widely used for its simplicity and versatility. It is suitable for developing web applications, scientific software, automation, data analysis, and much more.

6.1 Introduction to Python

What is Python?

Python is an interpreted programming language, meaning it is not compiled into machine code before execution. It is known for its simple and readable syntax, making it ideal for beginners.

How is Python Code Executed?

Python is interpreted and does not require compilation like traditional languages (e.g., C or Java). Instead, it is executed line by line using an interpreter.

Installing and Configuring the Development Environment

- **Download Python:** Visit python.org and download the latest version of Python.

Installation on Windows:

- Run the installation file.
- Ensure to check **"Add Python to PATH"** before clicking **"Install Now"**.

Installation on macOS:

Use the Homebrew package manager to install Python:

```
brew install python
```

Recommended Development Environment:

- **IDLE:** The built-in text editor included with Python.
- **Visual Studio Code:** A popular code editor with Python support (requires the Python extension).
- **PyCharm:** A powerful IDE designed for Python, suitable for complex projects.

Running Python Scripts from the Terminal

Running a Script:

Create a file named `script.py` with the following content:

```python
print("Hello, Python!")
```

Open the terminal (or command prompt), navigate to the file's folder, and type:

```
python script.py
```

Running Python Interactively:

Type `python` in the terminal to open the interactive interpreter.
Write and execute code line by line:

```
>>> print("Hello, World!")
Hello, World!
```

6.2 Basic Python

Syntax, Variables, and Data Types

Syntax:

Python uses indentation to define code blocks (instead of braces).
Example:

```python
if True:
  print("This is an indented block")
```

Variables:

Variables do not require type declarations.

```python
name = "Mario"  # String
age = 25        # Integer
pi = 3.14       # Float
```

- **Primitive Data Types:**

  - `int`: Integer numbers (e.g., `10`, `-5`).
  - `float`: Decimal numbers (e.g., `3.14`, `-0.5`).
  - `str`: Text strings (e.g., `"hello"`).
  - `bool`: Boolean values (`True` or `False`).

Control Structures: if, for, while

Conditional Statements (if):

```python
age = 18
if age >= 18:
    print("You are an adult")
else:
    print("You are a minor")
```

For Loops:

```python
for number in range(5):
  print(number)  # Prints numbers from 0 to 4
```

While Loops:

```
counter = 0
while counter < 5:
    print(counter)
    counter += 1
```

Functions, Scope, and Modules

Defining Functions:

```
def greet(name):
    return "Hello, " + name + "!"


print(greet("Luca"))  # "Hello, Luca!"
```

- **Variable Scope:**
  - **Local:** Variables declared inside a function.
  - **Global:** Variables declared outside any function.

```
name = "Anna"  # Global variable


def show_name():
    local_name = "Luca"  # Local variable
    print(local_name)


show_name()  # "Luca"
print(name)  # "Anna"
```

Importing Modules:
Python includes many built-in modules (e.g., math, os).

```
import math
print(math.sqrt(16))  # Square root of 16
```

6.3 Advanced Python

Object-Oriented Programming (OOP)

Classes and Objects:

```python
class Person:
    def __init__(self, name, age):
        self.name = name
        self.age = age

    def greet(self):
        print(f"Hello, my name is {self.name} and I am {self.age} years old")

person1 = Person("Giulia", 30)
person1.greet()
```

Inheritance:

```python
class Student(Person):
    def __init__(self, name, age, student_id):
        super().__init__(name, age)
        self.student_id = student_id

    def show_id(self):
        print(f"Student ID: {self.student_id}")

student = Student("Marco", 20, "12345")
student.greet()
student.show_id()
```

Exception Handling

Try, Except:

```
try:
    x = int(input("Enter a number: "))
    print(10 / x)
except ValueError:
    print("That's not a valid number!")
except ZeroDivisionError:
    print("You can't divide by zero!")
```

Working with Files, Input/Output

Reading and Writing Files:

```
# Writing to a file
with open("file.txt", "w") as file:
    file.write("Hello, file!\n")

# Reading from a file
with open("file.txt", "r") as file:
    content = file.read()
    print(content)
```

Standard Libraries

- **os:** Interacting with the operating system.

random: Generating random numbers.

```
import random
print(random.randint(1, 10))  # Random number between 1 and 10
```

datetime: Working with dates and times.

```
from datetime import datetime
print(datetime.now())  # Current date and time
```

6.4 All Python Built-in Functions and Modules

Python provides a comprehensive set of built-in functions that can be used without importing any modules. Here is a complete list:

Built-in Functions

Conversion Functions

- `abs(x)`: Returns the absolute value of `x`.
- `all(iterable)`: Returns `True` if all elements of the iterable are true.
- `any(iterable)`: Returns `True` if at least one element of the iterable is true.
- `ascii(object)`: Returns a readable representation of the object.
- `bin(x)`: Converts an integer to a binary string.
- `bool(x)`: Converts a value to a boolean.
- `bytearray([source[, encoding[, errors]]])`: Returns a `bytearray` object.
- `bytes([source[, encoding[, errors]]])`: Returns a `bytes` object.
- `chr(x)`: Returns the Unicode character for an integer.
- `complex(real, [imag])`: Creates a complex number.

Utility Functions

- `delattr(object, name)`: Deletes an attribute from an object.
- `dir([object])`: Returns a list of attributes and methods of an object.
- `divmod(a, b)`: Returns a tuple containing the quotient and remainder.
- `enumerate(iterable, start=0)`: Returns an enumerate object.
- `eval(expression)`: Evaluates a Python expression.
- `exec(object[, globals[, locals]])`: Executes a Python code object.
- `filter(function, iterable)`: Filters elements of an iterable.
- `format(value, format_spec)`: Formats a value.
- `getattr(object, name[, default])`: Gets the attribute of an object.
- `globals()`: Returns the global variables dictionary.
- `hasattr(object, name)`: Checks if an object has an attribute.
- `hash(object)`: Returns the hash value of an object.
- `help([object])`: Displays the interactive help text.
- `hex(x)`: Converts an integer to a hexadecimal string.
- `id(object)`: Returns the unique ID of an object.
- `input([prompt])`: Reads input from the user.
- `int(x[, base])`: Converts a value to an integer.
- `isinstance(object, classinfo)`: Checks if an object is an instance of a class.
- `issubclass(class, classinfo)`: Checks if a class is a subclass of another.
- `iter(object[, sentinel])`: Returns an iterator.

Collection and Iterable Functions

- `len(s)`: Returns the length of an object.
- `list([iterable])`: Creates a list.
- `map(function, iterable, ...)`: Applies a function to all elements of an iterable.
- `max(iterable, *[, key, default])`: Returns the maximum value.
- `min(iterable, *[, key, default])`: Returns the minimum value.
- `next(iterator[, default])`: Returns the next item of an iterator.
- `object()`: Returns a new base object.
- `oct(x)`: Converts an integer to an octal string.
- `open(file, mode='r', ...)`: Opens a file.
- `ord(c)`: Returns the Unicode value of a character.
- `pow(x, y[, z])`: Returns x raised to the power y.
- `print(*objects, sep=' ', end='\n', file=sys.stdout, flush=False)`: Prints a message.
- `property(fget=None, fset=None, fdel=None, doc=None)`: Returns a property.
- `range(start, stop[, step])`: Returns a sequence of numbers.
- `repr(object)`: Returns a string representation of an object.
- `reversed(seq)`: Returns an iterator that reverses the sequence.
- `round(number[, ndigits])`: Rounds a number.
- `set([iterable])`: Creates a set.
- `setattr(object, name, value)`: Sets an attribute of an object.
- `slice(start, stop[, step])`: Returns a `slice` object.
- `sorted(iterable, *, key=None, reverse=False)`: Returns a sorted list.
- `str(object='')`: Converts a value to a string.
- `sum(iterable, /, start=0)`: Sums the elements of an iterable.
- `tuple([iterable])`: Creates a tuple.
- `type(object)`: Returns the type of an object.
- `vars([object])`: Returns the `__dict__` attribute of an object.
- `zip(*iterables)`: Combines elements of iterables into tuples.

Python Standard Modules

Python's standard library offers a wide variety of modules for different functionalities.

Math and Statistics Modules

- `math`: Advanced mathematical operations.
- `cmath`: Operations on complex numbers.
- `decimal`: High-precision decimal arithmetic.
- `fractions`: Rational number arithmetic.
- `random`: Random number generation.
- `statistics`: Statistical functions.

Date and Time Modules

- `datetime`: Manipulation of dates and times.
- `time`: Time-related functions.
- `calendar`: Calendar operations.
- `zoneinfo`: Time zone information.

File and OS Modules

- `os`: Interaction with the operating system.
- `shutil`: File operations.
- `pathlib`: File path manipulation.
- `tempfile`: Creation of temporary files.
- `fnmatch`: File name pattern matching.
- `glob`: Finding files by pattern.
- `fileinput`: Iteration over input files.
- `pickle`: Serialization of Python objects.
- `json`: Reading and writing JSON data.
- `csv`: Reading and writing CSV files.

Exception Handling Modules

- `warnings`: Generate runtime warnings.
- `logging`: Log messages for debugging.

Networking and Internet Modules

- `socket`: Low-level network programming.
- `http`: HTTP protocol handling.
- `urllib`: URL manipulation.
- `ftplib`: FTP protocol interface.
- `email`: Email handling.

- `smtplib`: Sending emails.

Threading and Concurrency Modules

- `threading`: Multi-threaded programming.
- `multiprocessing`: Parallelism using processes.
- `concurrent.futures`: Asynchronous call execution.

Testing and Debugging Modules

- `unittest`: Unit testing framework.
- `doctest`: Test code written in documentation.
- `pdb`: Interactive debugger.

Miscellaneous Utilities

- `argparse`: Command-line argument parsing.
- `configparser`: Configuration file parsing.
- `subprocess`: Execute system commands.
- `re`: Regular expressions.
- `collections`: Advanced data containers (e.g., `deque`, `Counter`).
- `itertools`: Efficient iteration tools.
- `functools`: Functional programming tools.
- `operator`: Functional-style operators.

This list includes the most important built-in functions and standard modules in Python, useful for a wide range of projects.

Module 7: Front-End Frameworks (e.g., React, Vue, Angular)

Front-end frameworks like React, Vue, and Angular are powerful tools that facilitate the development of modern, interactive web applications. They enable the creation of reusable components, efficient state management, and seamless data interactions.

7.1 Introduction to Front-End Frameworks

Key Advantages and Use Cases

Key Advantages:
- **Reusable Components:** All three frameworks follow a component-based approach, making the code more organized and maintainable.
- **Efficient Updates:** They handle DOM updates efficiently using techniques like the Virtual DOM (used by React).
- **State Management:** Provide tools for clear and reactive state management.
- **Routing and Navigation:** Allow smooth navigation between pages or views without reloading the entire application.

Use Cases:
- **React:** Suitable for interactive web applications with complex client-side logic. Ideal for Single Page Applications (SPA) and large enterprise projects.
- **Vue:** Perfect for projects requiring quick setup and a gentler learning curve compared to Angular.
- **Angular:** Preferred for large-scale enterprise applications due to its comprehensive and robust structure.

Installation and Basic Setup

React:

Installation: Use `create-react-app` to set up a React project.

```
npx create-react-app project-name
cd project-name
npm start
```

- **Project Structure:** The `App.js` file is the starting point for your React application.

Vue:

Installation: Use Vue CLI to set up a Vue project.

```
npm install -g @vue/cli
vue create project-name
cd project-name
npm run serve
```

- **Project Structure:** The `App.vue` file is the root component of the application.

Angular:

Installation: Use Angular CLI to start a new Angular project.

```
npm install -g @angular/cli
ng new project-name
cd project-name
ng serve
```

- **Project Structure:** The `app.component.ts` file is Angular's main component.

7.2 Building Interactive Components

Components are the cornerstone of every front-end framework. Each component represents a reusable part of the user interface.

JSX (for React) or Templates (for Vue/Angular)

React with JSX:

JSX: A syntax similar to HTML used in React to describe the UI.

```
function Greeting() {
return <h1>Hello, World!</h1>;
}
```

Props: Properties passed to components to make them dynamic.

```
function Welcome(props) {
return <h1>Hello, {props.name}!</h1>;
}
```

Vue with Templates:

Template: HTML with Vue directives like `v-if` and `v-for`.

```
<template>
<div>
  <h1>{{ message }}</h1>
</div>
</template>
<script>
export default {
  data() {
    return {
      message: "Hello, World!"
    };
  }
};
</script>
```

Angular with Templates:

Template: HTML with Angular bindings and directives like `*ngIf` and `*ngFor`.

```
<h1 *ngIf="showTitle">{{ title }}</h1>
```

Components: Defined using TypeScript.

```
import { Component } from '@angular/core';

@Component({
  selector: 'app-greeting',
  template: '<h1>{{ title }}</h1>',
})
export class GreetingComponent {
  title = 'Hello, World!';
}
```

State Management and Props

React State Management:

```
import React, { useState } from 'react';

function Counter() {
  const [count, setCount] = useState(0);

  return (
    <div>
      <p>Count: {count}</p>
      <button onClick={() => setCount(count + 1)}>Increment</button>
    </div>
  );
}
```

Vue State Management:

```
<template>
<p>Count: {{ count }}</p>
<button @click="increment">Increment</button>
</template>
<script>
export default {
  data() {
    return {
      count: 0
    };
  },
  methods: {
    increment() {
      this.count++;
    }
  }
};
</script>
```

Angular State Management:

```
import { Component } from '@angular/core';

@Component({
  selector: 'app-counter',
  template: `
    <p>Count: {{ count }}</p>
    <button (click)="increment()">Increment</button>
  `,
})
export class CounterComponent {
  count = 0;
  increment() {
    this.count++;
  }
}
```

7.3 Advanced: Routing and Data Management

Front-end frameworks provide tools for managing navigation and data flow between components.

Navigation and Routing

React Routing:

```
import { BrowserRouter as Router, Route, Switch } from 'react-router-dom';

function App() {
  return (
    <Router>
      <Switch>
        <Route path="/" exact component={Home} />
        <Route path="/about" component={About} />
      </Switch>
    </Router>
  );
}
```

Vue Routing:

```javascript
  import Vue from 'vue';
import VueRouter from 'vue-router';
import Home from './components/Home.vue';
import About from './components/About.vue';

Vue.use(VueRouter);

const routes = [
  { path: '/', component: Home },
  { path: '/about', component: About }
];

const router = new VueRouter({ routes });

new Vue({
  router,
  render: h => h(App)
}).$mount('#app');
```

Angular Routing:

```javascript
  import { NgModule } from '@angular/core';
import { RouterModule, Routes } from '@angular/router';
import { HomeComponent } from './home/home.component';
import { AboutComponent } from './about/about.component';

const routes: Routes = [
  { path: '', component: HomeComponent },
  { path: 'about', component: AboutComponent }
];

@NgModule({
  imports: [RouterModule.forRoot(routes)],
  exports: [RouterModule]
})
export class AppRoutingModule {}
```

Data Management with API Integration

React API Fetching:

```javascript
import React, { useEffect, useState } from 'react';

function APIData() {
  const [data, setData] = useState([]);

  useEffect(() => {
    fetch('https://api.example.com/data')
      .then(response => response.json())
      .then(data => setData(data));
  }, []);

  return (
    <ul>
      {data.map(item => (
        <li key={item.id}>{item.name}</li>
      ))}
    </ul>
  );
}
```

Vue API Fetching:

```
<template>
<ul>
  <li v-for="item in data" :key="item.id">{{ item.name }}</li>
</ul>
</template>
<script>
export default {
  data() {
    return {
      data: []
    };
  },
  created() {
    fetch('https://api.example.com/data')
      .then(response => response.json())
      .then(data => (this.data = data));
  }
};
</script>
```

Angular API Fetching:

```typescript
import { Component, OnInit } from '@angular/core';
import { HttpClient } from '@angular/common/http';

@Component({
  selector: 'app-api-data',
  template: `
    <ul>
      <li *ngFor="let item of data">{{ item.name }}</li>
    </ul>
  `,
})
export class APIDataComponent implements OnInit {
  data: any[] = [];

  constructor(private http: HttpClient) {}

  ngOnInit() {
    this.http.get<any[]>('https://api.example.com/data')
      .subscribe(data => this.data = data);
  }
}
```

This module covers the foundational and advanced features of React, Vue, and Angular for developing dynamic and interactive web applications.

7.4 How to Integrate a Front-End Framework

1. Installing and Configuring React

Steps to Set Up React

Prerequisites:

- Ensure Node.js is installed on your computer. Download it from nodejs.org.

Create a New React Project:

Use `create-react-app`, an official tool for starting a React project without complex configurations.

```
npx create-react-app project-name
```

Notes:
- `npx` is a tool included with Node.js for running npm packages without globally installing them.
- Replace `project-name` with the name of your project folder.

Start the Project:

Navigate to the project folder:

```
cd project-name
```

Start the development server:

```
npm start
```

Your project will run at `http://localhost:3000` in your browser.

Project Structure:

- `src:` Contains source code files, such as components and CSS files.
- `public:` Contains the `index.html` file and static resources.
- The entry point for the project is `src/index.js`, and the main component is `src/App.js`.

2. Installing and Configuring Vue

Steps to Set Up Vue

Prerequisites:

- Ensure Node.js is installed on your computer.

Install Vue CLI:

Vue CLI is an official tool for generating and managing Vue projects.

```
npm install -g @vue/cli
```

Notes: The -g option installs Vue CLI globally on your system.

Create a New Vue Project:

Use Vue CLI to create a project:

```
vue create project-name
```

During setup, Vue CLI will prompt you to choose configurations. You can select default options or customize them.

Start the Project:

Navigate to the project folder:

```
cd project-name
```

Start the development server:

```
npm run serve
```

The project will be accessible at http://localhost:8080 in your browser.

Project Structure:

- **src:** Contains Vue components, the App.vue file, and the entry point main.js.
- **public:** Contains the index.html file and static resources.

3. Installing and Configuring Angular
Steps to Set Up Angular

Prerequisites:

- Ensure Node.js is installed on your computer.

Install Angular CLI:

Angular CLI is an official tool for creating and managing Angular projects.

```
npm install -g @angular/cli
```

Notes: The -g option installs Angular CLI globally.

Create a New Angular Project:

Use Angular CLI to create a project:

```
ng new project-name
```

Angular CLI will guide you through the setup process, asking if you want to include features like routing and which CSS style to use.

Start the Project:

Navigate to the project folder:

```
cd project-name
```

Start the development server:

```
ng serve
```

The project will be accessible at http://localhost:4200 in your browser.
Project Structure:

- src: Contains all project files, including components, services, and modules.
- app: A subfolder of src that includes app.component.ts, Angular's main component.

Tips for Choosing a Framework

React:

- **Advantages:** Easy to learn for those familiar with JavaScript. Suitable for projects requiring a custom structure.
- Ideal if you prefer flexibility and a component-based ecosystem.

Vue:

- **Advantages:** Easy to configure and highly versatile. Offers a gentler learning curve.
- Perfect for small-to-medium projects or rapid prototyping.

Angular:

- **Advantages:** Comprehensive structure and backed by Google. Excellent for large-scale enterprise applications.
- Recommended for those seeking a robust framework with many integrated features (e.g., routing, form validation).

Module 8: Back-End Programming Languages

Back-end programming manages the interaction between the front-end (what the user sees and uses) and the database or server. Back-end languages are responsible for logic, authentication, authorization, data management, and executing server-side operations.

8.1 Basic PHP

Introduction to PHP

PHP (Hypertext Preprocessor) is a server-side scripting language widely used for web application development. It is easy to learn and powerful for handling server-side logic, generating dynamic content, and interacting with databases.

Syntax, Variables, and Control Structures

Basic Syntax:

A PHP file is written within `<?php ... ?>` tags, and each statement ends with a semicolon `;`.
Example:

```php
<?php
echo "Hello, world!";
?>
```

- `echo`: Used to print something on the web page.

Variables:

Variables start with `$` and do not require type declarations (PHP is a dynamically typed language).

Example:

```php
<?php
$name = "Mario"; // String variable
$age = 30;       // Integer variable
$pi = 3.14;      // Float variable
echo "Hello, $name! You are $age years old.";
?>
```

Data Types in PHP:

1.   **Strings:** A sequence of characters enclosed in single or double quotes.
2.   **Integers:** Whole numbers.
3.   **Floats:** Decimal numbers.
4.   **Booleans:** true or false.
5.   **Arrays:** Container for multiple values.
6.   **Objects:** Representation of entities with properties and methods.

Control Structures:

1.   **Conditionals (if, else, elseif):**

```php
<?php
$hour = 15;
if ($hour < 12) {
    echo "Good morning!";
} elseif ($hour < 18) {
    echo "Good afternoon!";
} else {
    echo "Good evening!";
}
?>
```

2.   **Loops (for, while, do-while):**

For Loop:

```php
for ($i = 1; $i <= 5; $i++) {
    echo "Number: $i<br>";
}
```

While Loop:

```php
$j = 0;
while ($j < 5) {
    echo "Counter: $j<br>";
    $j++;
}
```

Do-While Loop:

```php
$k = 0;
do {
    echo "Value: $k<br>";
    $k++;
} while ($k < 3);
?>
```

Handling Forms and Sessions

Handling Data Submitted via Forms:

PHP can collect data from HTML forms using the superglobal arrays $_GET and $_POST.

Example:

```php
<?php
if ($_SERVER["REQUEST_METHOD"] == "POST") {
    $name = htmlspecialchars($_POST['name']); // Sanitize input
    echo "Hello, $name!";
}
?>
<!-- HTML Form -->
<form method="post" action="">
    Name: <input type="text" name="name">
    <input type="submit" value="Submit">
</form>
```

- **Sanitizing Data:** Use htmlspecialchars() to prevent XSS attacks.

Sessions in PHP:

Sessions allow you to maintain persistent information across pages.

Example:

```php
<?php
session_start(); // Start the session
$_SESSION['username'] = "Mario";
echo "Hello, " . $_SESSION['username'];
?>
```

Connecting to MySQL Databases

Connecting to a Database:

Use `mysqli` or `PDO` to connect to a MySQL database.
Example with `mysqli`:

```php
<?php
$conn    =    new    mysqli("localhost",    "username",    "password",
    "database_name");
if ($conn->connect_error) {
    die("Connection failed: " . $conn->connect_error);
}
echo "Connected successfully!";
?>
```

Executing Queries:

1.   **Selecting Data:**

```php
$query = "SELECT * FROM users";
$result = $conn->query($query);

if ($result->num_rows > 0) {
    while ($row = $result->fetch_assoc()) {
        echo "Name: " . $row["name"] . "<br>";
    }
} else {
    echo "No results found.";
}
```

8.2 Advanced PHP

Object-Oriented Programming (OOP)

PHP supports object-oriented programming (OOP), which includes concepts like classes, objects, inheritance, and encapsulation.

Defining Classes and Objects:

Example of a Class:

```php
class Automobile {
    public $brand;
    public $model;

    public function __construct($brand, $model) {
        $this->brand = $brand;
        $this->model = $model;
    }

    public function description() {
        return "Car: $this->brand $this->model";
    }
}

$car = new Automobile("Fiat", "500");
echo $car->description();
```

Inheritance:

Classes can extend other classes to inherit methods and properties.

Example:

```php
class Vehicle {
    protected $licensePlate;

    public function __construct($licensePlate) {
        $this->licensePlate = $licensePlate;
    }

    public function showLicensePlate() {
        return "License Plate: $this->licensePlate";
    }
}

class Motorcycle extends Vehicle {
    public $type;

    public function __construct($licensePlate, $type) {
        parent::__construct($licensePlate);
        $this->type = $type;
    }

    public function description() {
                return "Motorcycle $this->type with license plate
    $this->licensePlate";
    }
}

$motorcycle = new Motorcycle("AB123CD", "Sport");
echo $motorcycle->description();
```

Security: Validation and Protection

Input Validation:

Use `filter_var()` to validate emails, URLs, and other variables.

Example:

```php
$email = "test@example.com";
if (filter_var($email, FILTER_VALIDATE_EMAIL)) {
    echo "Valid email.";
} else {
    echo "Invalid email.";
}
```

SQL Injection Protection:

Use prepared statements with `mysqli` or PDO to avoid malicious code insertion.

Example with `mysqli`:

```php
$stmt = $conn->prepare("SELECT * FROM users WHERE name = ?");
$stmt->bind_param("s", $name);
$name = "Mario";
$stmt->execute();
$result = $stmt->get_result();
```

XSS Attack Prevention:

Use `htmlspecialchars()` to sanitize output against malicious JavaScript.

Example:

```php
$name = "<script>alert('XSS')</script>";
echo htmlspecialchars($name); // Safe output
```

PHP Frameworks (e.g., Laravel) and API Development

Laravel:

A modern PHP framework known for its simplicity and elegant structure.

Installation:

```
composer create-project --prefer-dist laravel/laravel project-name
```

Routes and Controllers:

```
Route::get('/user', 'UserController@index');
```

Use the following command to generate a controller:

```
php artisan make:controller UserController
```

Creating APIs with Laravel:

Use controllers to handle API requests and responses.

Example:

```
class UserController extends Controller {
    public function index() {
        return response()->json(['name' => 'Mario', 'age' => 30]);
    }
}
```

8.3 Introduction to Other Back-End Languages

Node.js and Server-Side JavaScript Runtime

Node.js is a JavaScript runtime environment that allows you to execute code on the server side. It is fast and efficient due to its event-driven, non-blocking I/O model.

Installing Node.js:
Download and install Node.js from nodejs.org.

Creating a Server with Express:
Express is a minimalist framework for web applications in Node.js.

Steps:

```
mkdir project-name
cd project-name
npm init -y
npm install express
```

Server Example:

```
const express = require('express');
const app = express();
const port = 3000;

app.get('/', (req, res) => {
    res.send('Hello, Node.js!');
});

app.listen(port, () => {
    console.log(`Server running at http://localhost:${port}`);
});
```

Python for the Web (Flask, Django)

Python is a versatile language used for web development, machine learning, and more.

Flask:

A simple and lightweight microframework.

Example:

```python
from flask import Flask
app = Flask(__name__)

@app.route("/")
def home():
    return "Hello, Flask!"

if __name__ == "__main__":
    app.run(debug=True)
```

Django:

A complete and robust framework for web development.

Creating a Project:

```
django-admin startproject project_name
cd project_name
python manage.py runserver
```

Example View:

```python
from django.http import HttpResponse

def greeting(request):
    return HttpResponse("Hello, Django!")
```

Ruby on Rails

Rails is a Ruby-based framework known for its productivity and the principle of "Convention over Configuration."

Installing Rails:

```
gem install rails
rails new project_name
cd project_name
rails server
```

Example Controller:

```
class WelcomeController < ApplicationController
  def greeting
    render plain: "Hello, Ruby on Rails!"
  end
end
```

Practical Exercises

Objective: Experiment with at least one additional back-end language, such as Node.js, Flask, or Rails.

Activities:

1.   **Build a Simple Application:** Create an app that responds with "Hello, World!" to demonstrate basic server setup.
2.   **Implement Routing:** Add routes to explore the basic functionalities of the chosen framework.

- ○   **For Node.js:** Create multiple `app.get()` routes.
- ○   **For Flask:** Define multiple `@app.route()` endpoints.
- ○   **For Rails:** Add methods in a controller and configure routes in `config/routes.rb`.

These exercises will help you explore the fundamental features of these back-end technologies.

Module 9: APIs and Web Services

9.1 What is an API and How Does it Work

Definition of API:

An API (Application Programming Interface) is an interface that allows two applications to communicate with each other. APIs enable structured and secure data exchange.

Types of APIs:

- **REST (Representational State Transfer):** An architectural style that uses HTTP for communication and supports methods like GET, POST, PUT, and DELETE.
- **SOAP (Simple Object Access Protocol):** A protocol based on XML, more complex and structured than REST.
- **GraphQL:** A query language for APIs that allows fetching precisely the data needed.

Example of How a REST API Works:

HTTP Request:

```
GET /api/users/1 HTTP/1.1
Host: api.example.com
```

HTTP Response:

```
{
  "id": 1,
  "name": "Mario Rossi",
  "email": "mario@example.com"
}
```

9.2 Creating REST APIs

Structure and Implementation

Structure of a REST API:

A REST API is based on resources. Each resource (e.g., users, products) has a specific endpoint.

Example: `/api/users`, `/api/products`

Implementing a REST API with Node.js and Express:

Basic Setup:

```
const express = require('express');
const app = express();
const port = 3000;

app.use(express.json()); // Middleware for handling request bodies

// Endpoint to get all users
app.get('/api/users', (req, res) => {
    res.json([{ id: 1, name: 'Mario' }, { id: 2, name: 'Luigi' }]);
});

// Endpoint to create a new user
app.post('/api/users', (req, res) => {
    const newUser = req.body;
    res.status(201).json(newUser); // Simulates user creation
});

app.listen(port, () => {
    console.log(`Server running at http://localhost:${port}`);
});
```

Best Practices for REST APIs:

1. Use appropriate HTTP status codes (e.g., `200 OK`, `201 Created`, `404 Not Found`).
2. Document the API using tools like **Swagger**.
3. Maintain a consistent response format (e.g., JSON).

API Security

Authentication and Authorization:

Use JWT (JSON Web Tokens) to authenticate users.

Example of JWT Token Generation:

```
const jwt = require('jsonwebtoken');
const token = jwt.sign({ id: 1, name: 'Mario' }, 'secret-key', {
  expiresIn: '1h' });
```

Protection Against Common Attacks:

- Always validate and sanitize user input.
- Use CORS (Cross-Origin Resource Sharing) to control who can access the API.

9.3 Consuming APIs

Using Third-Party APIs

Example with Fetch in JavaScript:

```javascript
fetch('https://api.example.com/data')
    .then(response => response.json())
    .then(data => console.log(data))
    .catch(error => console.error('Error:', error));
```

Example with Axios in Node.js:

```javascript
const axios = require('axios');

axios.get('https://api.example.com/data')
    .then(response => {
        console.log(response.data);
    })
    .catch(error => {
        console.error('Error:', error);
    });
```

Integration in Web Applications

Example of Integration with React:

Use `useEffect` to fetch data from an API and display it.

```
import React, { useEffect, useState } from 'react';

function App() {
    const [data, setData] = useState([]);

    useEffect(() => {
        fetch('https://api.example.com/data')
            .then(response => response.json())
            .then(data => setData(data))
            .catch(error => console.error('Error:', error));
    }, []);

    return (
        <div>
            <h1>Data List</h1>
            <ul>
                {data.map(item => (
                    <li key={item.id}>{item.name}</li>
                ))}
            </ul>
        </div>
    );
}

export default App;
```

This example demonstrates how to retrieve and display data from an API in a React application.

Module 10: Security and Performance

10.1 Key Web Vulnerabilities

XSS (Cross-Site Scripting)

Description: Attackers inject malicious JavaScript into a web page viewed by other users.
Prevention Example:

Use `htmlspecialchars()` in PHP to sanitize output:

```php
$name = "<script>alert('XSS');</script>";
echo htmlspecialchars($name); // Protects against XSS
```

CSRF (Cross-Site Request Forgery)

Description: Attackers trick an authenticated user into performing unauthorized actions.

Prevention Example:

Use CSRF tokens to secure forms.

> **Example with Laravel:** Laravel automatically includes CSRF protection in forms.

SQL Injection

Description: Attackers inject malicious SQL code through user input.

Prevention Example with Prepared Statements:

```php
$stmt = $conn->prepare("SELECT * FROM users WHERE name = ?");
$stmt->bind_param("s", $name);
$name = "Mario";
$stmt->execute();
```

Best Practices for Security

1. **Input Validation:** Always validate input on the server side.
2. **Secure Authentication:** Use protocols like OAuth2 or JWT.
3. **Regular Updates:** Keep software up-to-date to protect against known vulnerabilities.

10.2 Performance Optimization

Caching Techniques

- **Browser Cache:** Use HTTP headers to control caching.
- **Server-Side Cache:** Use tools like Redis or Memcached to store frequently requested data.

Image and File Optimization

- **Image Compression:** Use formats like WebP or compression tools.
- **Minification:** Reduce the size of CSS, JavaScript, and HTML files.

Example with Gulp:

```javascript
const gulp = require('gulp');
const cleanCSS = require('gulp-clean-css');

gulp.task('minify-css', () => {
    return gulp.src('src/*.css')
        .pipe(cleanCSS())
        .pipe(gulp.dest('dist'));
});
```

Content Delivery Networks (CDN)

Description: CDNs distribute content globally to reduce latency.
Example: Use services like Cloudflare or AWS CloudFront to serve static resources.

10.3 Monitoring and Debugging

Debugging Tools

- **Chrome DevTools:** Analyze your web application's performance.
- **Postman:** Test APIs interactively.

Performance Analysis

- **Lighthouse:** A Google tool for analyzing performance and SEO.
- **New Relic:** Advanced monitoring for application performance.

This module provides an overview of essential techniques and tools to ensure the security and optimal performance of your web applications.

Module 11: Deployment and Project Management

11.1 Code Versioning with Git

Essential Git Commands

Initialize a Repository:

```
git init
```

Clone a Repository:

```
git clone https://github.com/username/repo.git
```

Add Changes and Commit:

```
git add .
git commit -m "Description of changes"
```

Push to a Remote Repository:

```
git push origin main
```

Working with GitHub or GitLab

- **Create a New Repository:** Use the GitHub or GitLab interface.
- **Pull Request Management:** Have your code reviewed before integrating it into the main branch.

11.2 Deploying Web Applications

Cloud Services

- **AWS (Amazon Web Services):**
  - Use **EC2** for virtual servers and **S3** for storage.
  - **Example Deployment with EC2:**
  1. Create a new EC2 instance.
  2. Configure Apache/Nginx and upload your application files.

- **Heroku:**
  - Ideal for small to medium-sized applications.

Example Deployment:

```
heroku login
git push heroku main
```

- **Netlify:**
  - Perfect for static sites and front-end applications.
  - Configure automatic deployment by linking your GitHub repository.

Basic Server Configuration

- **Security:** Use firewalls (e.g., ufw on Ubuntu) and SSL certificates.
- **Optimization:** Enable Gzip compression and server-side caching.

11.3 DevOps for Web Projects

Introduction to CI/CD

- **Continuous Integration (CI):** Automates code verification and testing for every commit.
- **Continuous Deployment (CD):** Automatically releases code to production after passing tests.

Automating the Development Process

Example with GitHub Actions:

```
name: CI/CD Pipeline
on: [push]
jobs:
  build:
    runs-on: ubuntu-latest
    steps:
      - uses: actions/checkout@v2
      - name: Install dependencies
        run: npm install
      - name: Run tests
        run: npm test
```

This module covers the tools and strategies needed for effective code versioning, secure and efficient deployment, and automation of development processes to streamline project management.

Module 12: Complete Project: Library Management System

This module guides beginners in creating a web application for library management. It includes database design, front-end development, back-end development, and incorporates security and optimization techniques.

12.1 Project Analysis

Objective

Develop a web application that manages books, users, and loans. Key functionalities include:

- **Book Management:** Add, modify, delete, and view books.
- **User Management:** User registration, authentication, and profile management.
- **Loan Management:** Record loans with due dates and return dates.

12.2 Database Design

E/R Model (Entity/Relationship)

- **Entity: Books**
  - **Attributes:**
    - `id_book` (PK): Unique identifier for the book.
    - `title`: Title of the book.
    - `author`: Author of the book.
    - `genre`: Literary genre of the book.
    - `year_published`: Year the book was published.
    - `available` (BOOLEAN): Indicates if the book is available for loan.

- **Entity: Users**
  - **Attributes:**
    - `id_user` (PK): Unique identifier for the user.
    - `name`: Name of the user.
    - `email` (UNIQUE): Unique email address.
    - `password`: Encrypted password for security.
    - `registration_date`: Date when the user registered.

- **Entity: Loans**
  - **Attributes:**
    - `id_loan` (PK): Unique identifier for the loan.
    - `id_user` (FK): Reference to the user who borrowed the book.
    - `id_book` (FK): Reference to the borrowed book.
    - `loan_date`: Date the book was borrowed.
    - `due_date`: Due date for returning the book.
    - `return_date`: Date the book was returned (nullable).

12.3 Relational Schema

Database and Table Creation

The following SQL code creates the necessary tables with constraints:

```sql
CREATE DATABASE library_management;
USE library_management;

-- Books Table
CREATE TABLE Books (
    id_book INT AUTO_INCREMENT PRIMARY KEY,
    title VARCHAR(255) NOT NULL,
    author VARCHAR(100) NOT NULL,
    genre VARCHAR(50),
    year_published YEAR,
    available BOOLEAN DEFAULT TRUE
);

-- Users Table
CREATE TABLE Users (
    id_user INT AUTO_INCREMENT PRIMARY KEY,
    name VARCHAR(50) NOT NULL,
    email VARCHAR(100) UNIQUE NOT NULL,
    password VARCHAR(255) NOT NULL,
    registration_date TIMESTAMP DEFAULT CURRENT_TIMESTAMP
);

-- Loans Table
CREATE TABLE Loans (
    id_loan INT AUTO_INCREMENT PRIMARY KEY,
    id_user INT,
    id_book INT,
    loan_date DATE NOT NULL,
    due_date DATE NOT NULL,
    return_date DATE,
    FOREIGN KEY (id_user) REFERENCES Users(id_user),
    FOREIGN KEY (id_book) REFERENCES Books(id_book)
);
```

12.4 Front-End Design

Registration Page (`registration.html`)

```html
<!DOCTYPE html>
<html lang="en">
<head>
    <meta charset="UTF-8">
            <meta    name="viewport"    content="width=device-width,
  initial-scale=1.0">
    <title>User Registration</title>
    <link rel="stylesheet" href="style.css">
</head>
<body>
    <div class="container">
        <h1>Register</h1>
        <form action="backend/register.php" method="POST">
            <label for="name">Name:</label>
            <input type="text" id="name" name="name" required>

            <label for="email">Email:</label>
            <input type="email" id="email" name="email" required>

            <label for="password">Password:</label>
                <input type="password" id="password" name="password"
  required>
            <button type="submit">Register</button>
        </form>
    </div>
</body>
</html>
```

Login Page (`login.html`)

```html
<!DOCTYPE html>
<html lang="en">
<head>
    <meta charset="UTF-8">
            <meta    name="viewport"    content="width=device-width,
  initial-scale=1.0">
    <title>User Login</title>
    <link rel="stylesheet" href="style.css">
</head>
<body>
    <div class="container">
        <h1>Login</h1>
        <form action="backend/login.php" method="POST">
            <label for="email">Email:</label>
            <input type="email" id="email" name="email" required>

            <label for="password">Password:</label>
                <input type="password" id="password" name="password"
  required>

            <button type="submit">Login</button>
        </form>
    </div>
</body>
</html>
```

CSS Styling (`style.css`)

```css
/* General styles for the page */
body {
    font-family: Arial, sans-serif;
    background-color: #f0f0f0;
    margin: 0;
    padding: 20px;
    display: flex;
    justify-content: center;
    align-items: center;
    min-height: 100vh;
}

/* Container styles */
.container {
    background-color: white;
    padding: 20px;
    border-radius: 5px;
    box-shadow: 0 0 10px rgba(0, 0, 0, 0.1);
    max-width: 400px;
    width: 100%;
}

h1 {
    text-align: center;
    margin-bottom: 20px;
}

label {
    display: block;
    margin-top: 10px;
}

input {
    width: 100%;
    padding: 8px;
    margin-top: 5px;
    border: 1px solid #ccc;
    border-radius: 4px;
}
```

```
button {
    width: 100%;
    padding: 10px;
    background-color: #28a745;
    color: white;
    border: none;
    border-radius: 4px;
    cursor: pointer;
    margin-top: 10px;
}

button:hover {
    background-color: #218838;
}
```

This module provides a comprehensive guide to building a library management system, covering database design, front-end development, and integration with back-end services.

12.5 Back-End Development

Database Connection (`connessione.php`)

```php
<?php
// Database connection configuration
$host = 'localhost';
$user = 'root';
$password = '';
$database = 'gestione_biblioteca';

// Create the connection
$conn = new mysqli($host, $user, $password, $database);

// Check the connection
if ($conn->connect_error) {
    die("Database connection failed: " . $conn->connect_error); //
  Error message on failure
}
?>
```

User Registration (`registrazione.php`)

```php
<?php
// Include database connection file
include 'connessione.php';

// Check if the request method is POST
if ($_SERVER['REQUEST_METHOD'] === 'POST') {
    // Sanitize input to prevent XSS attacks
    $nome = htmlspecialchars($_POST['nome']);
    $email = htmlspecialchars($_POST['email']);
    // Hash the password to protect user credentials
    $password = password_hash($_POST['password'], PASSWORD_BCRYPT);

    // Prepare the query to prevent SQL Injection
    $stmt = $conn->prepare("INSERT INTO Utenti (nome, email, password)
  VALUES (?, ?, ?)");
    $stmt->bind_param("sss", $nome, $email, $password);

    // Execute the query and check the result
    if ($stmt->execute()) {
        echo "Registration successful!";
    } else {
        echo "Error: " . $stmt->error; // Error message on failure
    }

    // Close the statement and connection
    $stmt->close();
    $conn->close();
}
?>
```

Explanation
- `htmlspecialchars()`: Converts special characters to HTML entities to prevent XSS attacks.
- `password_hash()`: Encrypts passwords using the BCRYPT algorithm for secure storage.
- **Prepared Statements**: Used to protect the database from SQL Injection attacks.

User Login (`login.php`)

```php
<?php
// Include database connection file
include 'connessione.php';
session_start(); // Start a session to keep the user authenticated

// Check if the request method is POST
if ($_SERVER['REQUEST_METHOD'] === 'POST') {
    // Sanitize input to prevent XSS attacks
    $email = htmlspecialchars($_POST['email']);
    $password = $_POST['password'];

 // Prepare the query to prevent SQL Injection
    $stmt = $conn->prepare("SELECT id_utente, nome, password FROM Utenti
 WHERE email = ?");
    $stmt->bind_param("s", $email);
    $stmt->execute();
    $result = $stmt->get_result();

 // Check if a user with the provided email exists
    if ($result->num_rows === 1) {
        $utente = $result->fetch_assoc();
        // Verify the entered password against the stored hash
        if (password_verify($password, $utente['password'])) {
            // Save user data in the session
            $_SESSION['id_utente'] = $utente['id_utente'];
            $_SESSION['nome'] = $utente['nome'];
            echo "Welcome, " . $_SESSION['nome'];
        } else {
            echo "Incorrect password."; // Error message for incorrect
 password
        }
    } else {
        echo "User not found."; // Error message if email is not registered
    }

 // Close the statement and connection
    $stmt->close();
    $conn->close();
}
?>
```

Explanation
-       `session_start()`: Starts or resumes an existing session, essential for keeping the user logged in.
-       `password_verify()`: Compares the entered password with the stored hash.

12.6 Data Security

Protection Against SQL Injection

SQL Injection involves injecting malicious SQL code through user inputs. To secure the application:

- Use **Prepared Statements** to separate SQL commands from user input.
  - Example: `$stmt->bind_param("s", $email);` binds user input safely.

Protection Against XSS (Cross-Site Scripting)

XSS allows attackers to execute malicious scripts in another user's browser.
- Use `htmlspecialchars()` to sanitize input and prevent execution of HTML or JavaScript code.

Password Hashing

User passwords must be encrypted to protect user data in case of a database breach.
- `password_hash()`: Creates a secure hash.
- `password_verify()`: Validates the entered password against the stored hash.

12.7 Performance Optimization

Caching

Caching reduces server load and speeds up response times.
- Use HTTP headers to cache pages:

```php
header("Cache-Control: max-age=3600"); // Cache for 1 hour
```

File Compression

Compress HTML, CSS, and JavaScript files to improve load times.
- Enable Gzip compression in PHP:

```php
ob_start("ob_gzhandler");
```

Minification

Minification removes unnecessary spaces and comments from CSS/JavaScript files.
- Use tools like CSS Minifier to reduce file size.

12.8 Deployment and Configuration

Deployment on a Secure Server

1.   Choose a reliable hosting provider, such as **AWS**, **Heroku**, or a **VPS**.
2.   Configure **HTTPS** using an SSL certificate to secure communications.

Backup and Restoration

Implement regular database backups to protect data.
*   Example of a MySQL backup:

```
mysqldump -u root -p gestione_biblioteca > backup.sql
```

This ensures data safety and enables recovery in case of system failures.

12.9 Complete Project Code: Library Management System

1. Database Connection File (`connessione.php`)

```php
<?php
// Database connection configuration
$host = 'localhost';
$user = 'root';
$password = '';
$database = 'gestione_biblioteca';

// Create the connection
$conn = new mysqli($host, $user, $password, $database);

// Check the connection
if ($conn->connect_error) {
    die("Database connection failed: " . $conn->connect_error);
}
?>
```

2. User Registration File (`registrazione.php`)

```php
<?php
// Include database connection file
include 'connessione.php';

// Check if the request method is POST
if ($_SERVER['REQUEST_METHOD'] === 'POST') {
    $nome = htmlspecialchars($_POST['nome']);
    $email = htmlspecialchars($_POST['email']);
    $password = password_hash($_POST['password'], PASSWORD_BCRYPT);

    // Prepared statement to prevent SQL Injection
    $stmt = $conn->prepare("INSERT INTO Utenti (nome, email, password)
  VALUES (?, ?, ?)");
    $stmt->bind_param("sss", $nome, $email, $password);

    // Execute the query
    if ($stmt->execute()) {
        echo "Registration successful!";
    } else {
        echo "Error: " . $stmt->error;
    }

    $stmt->close();
    $conn->close();
}
?>
```

3. User Login File (`login.php`)

```php
<?php
// Include database connection file
include 'connessione.php';
session_start(); // Start a session to keep the user authenticated

if ($_SERVER['REQUEST_METHOD'] === 'POST') {
    $email = htmlspecialchars($_POST['email']);
    $password = $_POST['password'];

    // Prepared statement to prevent SQL Injection
      $stmt = $conn->prepare("SELECT id_utente, nome, password FROM
  Utenti WHERE email = ?");
    $stmt->bind_param("s", $email);
    $stmt->execute();
    $result = $stmt->get_result();

    if ($result->num_rows === 1) {
        $utente = $result->fetch_assoc();
        if (password_verify($password, $utente['password'])) {
            $_SESSION['id_utente'] = $utente['id_utente'];
            $_SESSION['nome'] = $utente['nome'];
            echo "Welcome, " . $_SESSION['nome'];
        } else {
            echo "Incorrect password.";
        }
    } else {
        echo "User not found.";
    }

    $stmt->close();
    $conn->close();
}
?>
```

4. CSS File (`stile.css`)

```css
body {
    font-family: Arial, sans-serif;
    background-color: #f0f0f0;
    margin: 0;
    padding: 20px;
    display: flex;
    justify-content: center;
    align-items: center;
    min-height: 100vh;
}

.container {
    background-color: white;
    padding: 20px;
    border-radius: 5px;
    box-shadow: 0 0 10px rgba(0, 0, 0, 0.1);
    max-width: 400px;
    width: 100%;
}

h1 {
    text-align: center;
    margin-bottom: 20px;
}

label {
    display: block;
    margin-top: 10px;
}

input {
    width: 100%;
    padding: 8px;
    margin-top: 5px;
    border: 1px solid #ccc;
    border-radius: 4px;
}
```

```css
button {
    width: 100%;
    padding: 10px;
    background-color: #28a745;
    color: white;
    border: none;
    border-radius: 4px;
    cursor: pointer;
    margin-top: 10px;
}

button:hover {
    background-color: #218838;
}
```

5. Registration Page (`registrazione.html`)

```html
<!DOCTYPE html>
<html lang="en">
<head>
    <meta charset="UTF-8">
            <meta    name="viewport"    content="width=device-width,
  initial-scale=1.0">
    <title>User Registration</title>
    <link rel="stylesheet" href="stile.css">
</head>
<body>
    <div class="container">
        <h1>Register</h1>
        <form action="backend/registrazione.php" method="POST">
            <label for="nome">Name:</label>
            <input type="text" id="nome" name="nome" required>

            <label for="email">Email:</label>
            <input type="email" id="email" name="email" required>

            <label for="password">Password:</label>
                <input  type="password"  id="password"  name="password"
  required>

            <button type="submit">Register</button>
        </form>
    </div>
</body>
</html>
```

6. Login Page (`login.html`)

```html
<!DOCTYPE html>
<html lang="en">
<head>
    <meta charset="UTF-8">
                <meta    name="viewport"    content="width=device-width,
  initial-scale=1.0">
    <title>User Login</title>
    <link rel="stylesheet" href="stile.css">
</head>
<body>
    <div class="container">
        <h1>Login</h1>
        <form action="backend/login.php" method="POST">
            <label for="email">Email:</label>
            <input type="email" id="email" name="email" required>

            <label for="password">Password:</label>
                <input  type="password"  id="password"  name="password"
  required>

            <button type="submit">Login</button>
        </form>
    </div>
</body>
</html>
```

7. SQL Script to Create Database

```sql
CREATE DATABASE gestione_biblioteca;
USE gestione_biblioteca;

-- Table: Books
CREATE TABLE Libri (
    id_libro INT AUTO_INCREMENT PRIMARY KEY,
    titolo VARCHAR(255) NOT NULL,
    autore VARCHAR(100) NOT NULL,
    genere VARCHAR(50),
    anno_pubblicazione YEAR,
    disponibile BOOLEAN DEFAULT TRUE
);

-- Table: Users
CREATE TABLE Utenti (
    id_utente INT AUTO_INCREMENT PRIMARY KEY,
    nome VARCHAR(50) NOT NULL,
    email VARCHAR(100) UNIQUE NOT NULL,
    password VARCHAR(255) NOT NULL,
    data_registrazione TIMESTAMP DEFAULT CURRENT_TIMESTAMP
);

-- Table: Loans
CREATE TABLE Prestiti (
    id_prestito INT AUTO_INCREMENT PRIMARY KEY,
    id_utente INT,
    id_libro INT,
    data_prestito DATE NOT NULL,
    data_scadenza DATE NOT NULL,
    data_ritorno DATE,
    FOREIGN KEY (id_utente) REFERENCES Utenti(id_utente),
    FOREIGN KEY (id_libro) REFERENCES Libri(id_libro)
);
```

12.10 How the Structure Works

HTML Pages:

- Users access the HTML pages to register or log in.
- These pages contain forms that send data to the server via the POST method.

PHP Files:

- When the user submits the form, the data is sent to the corresponding PHP files (registrazione.php or login.php).
- These PHP files process the requests, interact with the database, and return a response to the user.

Flow Explanation

Registration:

1. The user fills out the form in registrazione.html.
2. The form sends the data to registrazione.php for processing.
3. registrazione.php:
   - Ensures security by sanitizing input.
   - Saves the data in the database.
   - Returns a message to the user about the registration status.

Login:

1. The user fills out the form in login.html.
2. The form sends the data to login.php for authentication.
3. login.php:
   - Verifies the provided credentials against the database.
   - If successful, manages the user's session.
   - Returns a welcome message or an error message.

Recommended Folder Structure

To keep the project organized, the following structure is suggested:

```
/gestione_biblioteca
|
├── /backend
|   ├── connessione.php
|   ├── registrazione.php
|   └── login.php
|
├── /frontend
|   ├── registrazione.html
|   ├── login.html
|   └── stile.css
|
└── /database
    └── script_creazione_tabelle.sql
```

Folder Purposes:

- **/backend**: Contains PHP files responsible for server-side logic.
- **/frontend**: Contains HTML and CSS files for the user interface.
- **/database**: Includes the SQL script to create the database and its tables.

Why Use Separate Pages?

1. **Organization**:
   - Separating HTML, CSS, and PHP makes the project easier to read and maintain.

2. **Security**:
   - PHP files handling server logic should not be directly accessible by the browser (except those explicitly processing requests), protecting the server-side code.

3. **Scalability**:
   - It becomes easier to add new features or modify parts of the project without affecting other components.

Module 13: Glossary

API (Application Programming Interface): A set of rules that allows different applications to communicate with each other. APIs simplify the integration of external features (e.g., a payment service) into your software.

Back-End: The part of a web application that manages logic, databases, and server interactions. It operates "behind the scenes" and is not visible to users.

Client-Server: An architecture where the client (e.g., a web browser) sends requests to a server, which responds by providing the requested data or processing.

CSS (Cascading Style Sheets): A style language used to define the appearance and layout of a web page written in HTML. It controls colors, fonts, spacing, and more.

DOM (Document Object Model): A structured representation of an HTML page that allows JavaScript to access and manipulate page elements.

Front-End: The visible part of a website or application that users interact with directly. It includes HTML, CSS, and JavaScript.

HTML (HyperText Markup Language): The standard markup language for creating web pages. It uses tags to structure content such as headings, paragraphs, images, links, and more.

JavaScript: A programming language used to make web pages interactive. It enables the creation of dynamic elements such as animations, real-time form validation, and content updates without reloading the page.

MySQL: An open-source relational database management system used to store and manage data for web applications.

PHP (Hypertext Preprocessor): A server-side scripting language used to create dynamic web pages. It runs on the server, and the output is sent to the user's browser.

SQL (Structured Query Language): A standard language used to query and manipulate databases. It supports operations such as retrieving, inserting, updating, and deleting data.

CSRF Token (Cross-Site Request Forgery Token): A security measure that prevents a malicious site from sending unauthorized requests to an application where the user is authenticated.

UI (User Interface): The interface of an application that includes everything the user interacts with, such as buttons, forms, and menus.

UX (User Experience): The overall experience a user has with an application or website, including factors like ease of use, speed, and overall satisfaction.

Version Control: A system that tracks changes to code so they can be rolled back or collaborated on with other developers. Git is one of the most popular version control tools.

Web App: An application accessible via a web browser that often interacts with a server to provide dynamic functionalities to users.

www.ingramcontent.com/pod-product-compliance
Lightning Source LLC
LaVergne TN
LVHW060123070326
832902LV00019B/3111